Garfield's WORST JOKES

By Mark Acey and Scott Nickel

Garfield created by JIM DAVIS

LERNER PUBLICATIONS ◆ MINNEAPOLIS

Did you hear the one about Garfield's burp? It brought down the house!

Copyright © 2021 by Paws, Inc. All Rights Reserved. "GARFIELD" and the GARFIELD characters are trademarks of Paws, Inc.
Based on the Garfield® characters created by Jim Davis

Nickelodeon is a Trademark of Viacom International Inc.

Visit Garfield online at https://www.garfield.com

Lerner Publications Company
An imprint of Lerner Publishing Group, Inc.
241 First Avenue North
Minneapolis, MN 55401 USA

For reading levels and more information, look up this title at www.lernerbooks.com.

Main body text set in Mikado a Bold.
Typeface provided by HVD fonts.

Editor: Allison Juda **Designer:** Susan Rouleau-Fienhage

Library of Congress Cataloging-in-Publication Data

The Cataloging-in-Publication Data for *Garfield's Worst Jokes* is on file at the Library of Congress.
ISBN 978-1-5415-8985-8 (lib. bdg.)
ISBN 978-1-72841-349-5 (pbk.)
ISBN 978-1-72840-028-0 (eb pdf)

Manufactured in the United States of America
1-47495-48039-1/23/2020

How do you drive Odie crazy?

Put him in a round room and tell him to go stand in the corner!

Did you hear about the cow who couldn't give milk?

She was an udder failure!

Why did the boy hold his report card over his head?

He was trying to raise his grades.

What grade is Garfield in?

The furrst grade!

How many sides does a triangle have?

Two. An inside and an outside.

WHAT? ISN'T THAT RIGHT?

**Why is the
shark so smart?**

He just ate a
school of fish!

**Why were the teacher's
eyes shining?**

Because she had
bright pupils!

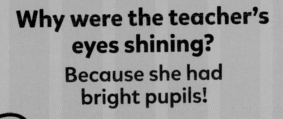

"Are you a serious soccer player?"

"No, I just play for kicks."

"I've been swimming since I was five years old."

"Gosh, you must be exhausted!"

ANOTHER EXCUSE TO SLEEP? I'LL TAKE IT!

What would you get if you crossed two fish with two elephants?
A pair of swimming trunks!

What does Garfield most like to catch?
A meatball.

KNOCK, KNOCK.

Who's there?

Noah.

Noah who?

Noah body . . . April Fool's!

What do you get if you cross Odie with a prankster's holiday?

April Drool's Day!

Does Garfield know all about April 1?
Yes, he's fooly aware of it!

GUESS WHO?

KNOCK, KNOCK.
Who's there?
Noah.
Noah who?
Noah something? It's still April Fool's!

I AM NOT AMUSED

Why does Garfield take extra naps on June 19?
Because he likes to have a nappy birthday!

What does Garfield always get on his birthday?
Another year older!

Why do we put candles on top of a birthday cake?
Because it's too hard to put them on the bottom!

Why did Odie put the cake in the freezer?
Because Jon told him to ice it.

What does Garfield get after he's eaten too much ice cream?
More ice cream!

DON'T I DESERVE IT!?

Why did the farmer take a baseball bat out to the barn?

His wife said it was time to hit the hay!

Why did the pig say "Cock-a-doodle-doo"?

Because it was the rooster's day off.

Why did the farmer jiggle the cow?

He was trying to make a milkshake!

What does a flock of tough sheep say?

"We're baaaa-d!"

THAT JOKE WAS BAAAD

KNOCK, KNOCK.

Who's there?

Matty.

Matty who?

Matty nice of you to invite me in!

IT WOULD BE EVEN NICER IF YOU'D INVITE ME TO YOUR DINNER TABLE!

KNOCK, KNOCK.

Who's there?
Wanda.
Wanda who?
Wanda drop by to say "hi!"

KNOCK, KNOCK.

Who's there?
Brad.
Brad who?
Brad news! Nermal's coming to visit!

World's Cutest Kitten

What kind of music does a leprechaun band play?
Shamrock 'n' roll!

Did you hear about the leprechaun who went to jail?
He was a leprecon!

KNOCK, KNOCK.

Who's there?
Irish.
Irish who?
Irish you a happy St. Patrick's Day!

Why can't Odie march in the St. Patrick's Day parade?
Because he can't march and breathe at the same time.

What would you get if you crossed a dog with an Irish instrument?
A bagpup!

IF WE COULD ONLY GET A PUP TO STAY IN A BAG . . .

Why did the pig give his girlfriend a box of candy?

It was Valenswine's Day!

What did the boy firefly say to the girl firefly?

"I really glow for you!"

What do you call it when dogs kiss?

A pooch smooch!

Is Garfield a light sleeper?
Yes, but he'd rather sleep in the dark.

The only active thing about Garfield is his imagination!

Why does Garfield attack the mail carriers?
He doesn't think dogs should have all the fun!

Garfield is so slow, he can't even catch a cold!

Did you hear the one about Odie?
It's a no-brainer!

huh?

Did you hear the one about the toothache?
It's a pain!

Did you hear the one about Odie's tongue?
It's a mouthful!

Did you hear the one about the lasagna?
It was panned!

I'D LIKE TO GET INTO THAT PAN!

What did the baseball glove say to the baseball?
"Catch you later!"

When is a hockey player like a magician?
When he does a hat trick.

How is Garfield like a basketball?
They're both round, orange, and frequently stuffed!

What football position is Garfield most likely to play?
Wide resleeper.

Z

Garfield's idea of exercise is a brisk two-hour nap!

Garfield was sick, so he went to the vet. And now he's feline fine!

I WAS FEELING FINE UNTIL I HEARD THAT TERRIBLE JOKE

Garfield is so lazy that he hired someone to breathe for him!

Garfield doesn't spend his whole day lying in bed. He also lies on the couch!

Why did the pitcher take a blanket onto the baseball field?

In case he had to cover first base.

What did the bowling ball say to the bowling pins?

"Don't stop me. I'm on a roll!"

ME TOO!

Why were the police staking out the baseball field?
They heard players were stealing bases.

Why is it hard to nap during a tennis match?
Because of all the racquet!

Why is it so hard to drive a golf ball?

Because it doesn't have a steering wheel.

DUH!

Why can't Garfield play in the NBA?

For Pete's sake, he's a cat!

Where do baseball players eat?
Home plate!

Why doesn't Garfield play basketball?
He shoots too many hair balls!

Did you hear the one about the floor?
It's beneath you!

Did you hear the one about the skunk?
It stinks!

JUST LIKE THE JOKES IN THIS BOOK!